Contents

Wharton Wristers 2	Peabody Hat and Mitts 20
One-Stitch Mug Cozy 3	Lila Bobble Cowl 22
Super Chunky Cowl 4	Pop of Color Garland 24
Rue Royale Beret 6	Hooded Scarf with Pockets 26
Coney Island Frank Dog Toy 8	The Poet Dog Sweater 28
Destin Beach Sun Hat 10	Crochet Soap Sack 31
Trenton Tote 12	Fenwick Scarf 32
Tenafly Scarf 15	Heige Hat 34
One-Ball Bobble Cowl 16	Shell-Stitch Cowl 36
Kent Street Bagel Cat Toy 18	Cozy Crochet Slippers 38

3

6

12

16

20

28

32

38

Wharton Wristers

Basic

MEASUREMENTS
Circumference Approx 7"/18cm
Length Approx 7 (12)"/(18 (30.5)cm
Note Pattern is written for shorter length with changes for longer length in parentheses. When only one number is given, it applies to both lengths.

MATERIALS
Yarn
LION BRAND® Wool-Ease®, Thick & Quick®, 6oz/170g balls; each approx 106yd/97m (acrylic, wool)
- 1 ball in #178 Cilantro or #189 Butterscotch

Hook
- Size M/13 (9mm) crochet hook, *or size needed to obtain gauge*

Notions
- Tapestry needle

GAUGE
7 stitches and 8 rows = 4"/10cm in hdc using size M/13 (9mm) hook.
TAKE TIME TO CHECK GAUGE.

WRISTERS (Make 2)
Ch 14.
Row 1 Hdc in 3rd chain from hook, hdc in each chain across.
Row 2 Ch 2, turn, hdc in each st across.
Rep Row 2 until piece measures approx 7 (12)"/(18 (30.5)cm from beg.
Fasten off.

FINISHING
Beg at top edge, sew side edges together for 1"/2.5cm, leave next 1½"/4cm open for thumb, sew remainder of side edges together. Weave in ends. •

One-Stitch Mug Cozy

Basic

MEASUREMENTS
Circumference Approx 9½"/24cm, to fit a standard coffee or tea mug
Height Approx 3½"/9cm

MATERIALS
Yarn
LION BRAND® Heartland®, 5 oz/142g balls; each 251yd/230m (acrylic, rayon) 〔4〕
• 1 ball in #105 Glacier Bay
Note Yarn amount is sufficient to make 4–5 Cozies.

Hook
• Size J/10 (6mm) crochet hook, *or size needed to obtain gauge*

Notions
• Tapestry needle
• One small button
• Sewing needle and thread

GAUGE
12 half double crochet and 10 rows = 4"/10cm using size J10 (6mm) hook. *TAKE TIME TO CHECK GAUGE.*

COZY
Ch 32.
Row 1 Hdc in 3rd ch from hook and in each ch across.
Row 2 Ch 2, turn. Hdc in each st across—29 sts at the end of this row.
Rep Row 2 until piece measures approx 3½"/9cm.
Fasten off.

FINISHING
Sew short sides of Cozy together for about ½"/1.5cm at top and at bottom, leaving rem 2½"/6.5cm open for mug handle.
With sewing needle and thread, sew button, centered, onto one edge of handle opening. Use spaces between sts as buttonhole. •

Super Chunky Cowl

Easy

MEASUREMENTS
Circumference About 34"/86.5cm
Height About 12"/30.5cm

MATERIALS
Yarn
LION BRAND® Hometown®, 5oz/142g balls; each 81yd/74m (acrylic)
- 1 ball in #150 Chicago Charcoal (A)
- 1 ball in #225 Springfield Silver (B)
- 1 ball in #226 Fayetteville Frost (C)

Hook
- Size P (15mm) crochet hook, *or size needed to obtain gauge.*

Notions
- Tapestry needle

GAUGE
4 pattern reps = 5"/12.5cm over Rnds 1–4 of pattern using size P (15mm) hook.
Note Each pattern rep consists of a puff and the following ch-1 sp. *TAKE TIME TO CHECK GAUGE.*

STITCH GLOSSARY
beg-puff (beginning puff) Ch 2, yarn over, insert hook in indicated st and draw up a loop (3 loops on hook), yarn over, insert hook in same st and draw up a loop, yarn over and draw through all 5 loops on hook.
puff Yarn over, insert hook in indicated st and draw up a loop (3 loops on hook), (yarn over, insert hook in same st and draw up a loop) twice, yarn over and draw through all 7 loops on hook.

NOTES
1) Cowl is worked in joined rnds with RS always facing.
2) Cowl is worked with 3 colors of yarn to make stripes.
3) If you find it difficult to join the beg ch into a ring without twisting the ch, Rnd 1 can be worked as a row, then joined into a rnd, as follows: Leaving a long beg tail, ch 56, yarn over, insert hook in 3rd ch from hook and draw up a loop (2 skipped ch count as ch 2 of beg-puff), yarn over, insert hook in same ch and draw up a loop, yarn over and draw through all 5 loops on hook (beg-puff made), *ch 1, sk next ch, puff in next ch; rep from * to last ch, ch 1, sk last ch; join with sl st in top of beg-puff—you will have 27 puffs and 27 ch-1 sps in this row/rnd. Use beg tail to sew gap at base of first row closed. Proceed to Rnd 2.
4) For those who find a visual helpful, we have included a stitch diagram.

COWL
With A, ch 54. Taking care not to twist ch, join with sl st in first ch to make a ring.
Rnd 1 (RS) Beg-puff in same ch as join, *ch 1, sk next ch, puff in next ch; rep from * to last ch, ch 1, sk last ch; join with sl st in top of beg-puff—you will have 27 pattern reps in this rnd.
Rnds 2–4 (Sl st, beg-puff) in first ch-1 sp, *ch 1, sk next puff, puff in next ch-1 sp; rep from * to last puff, ch 1, sk last puff; join with sl st in top of beg-puff.
Fasten off A.
Rnd 5 From RS, draw up a loop of B in first ch-1 sp, beg-puff in same ch-1 sp, *ch 1, sk next puff, puff in next ch-1 sp; rep from * to last puff, ch 1, sk last puff; join with sl st in top of beg-puff.
Rnds 6–8 With B, rep Rnds 2–4.
Fasten off B.
Rnds 9–12 With C, rep Rnds 5–8.
Fasten off C.

FINISHING
Weave in ends. •

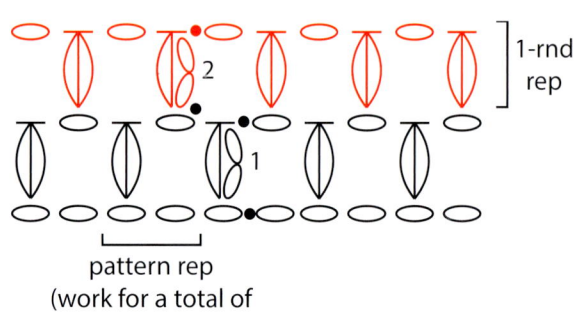

pattern rep
(work for a total of 27 reps)

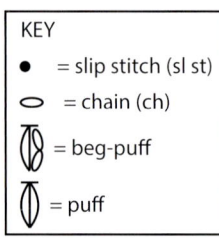

Rue Royale Beret

Easy

MEASUREMENTS
Circumference at Lower Edge Approx 19"/48.5cm; will stretch to fit a range of sizes

MATERIALS
Yarn
LION BRAND® Mandala® Tweed Stripes®, 5.3oz/150g balls; each 426yd/390m (acrylic) (4)
• 1 ball in #220 Dragonfly

Hook
• Size H/8 (5mm) crochet hook, *or size needed to obtain gauge.*

Notions
• Tapestry needle

GAUGE
15 sc = 5"/12.5cm using size H/8 (5mm) hook.
TAKE TIME TO CHECK GAUGE.

STITCH GLOSSARY
sc2tog (sc 2 sts together) (Insert hook in next st and draw up a loop) twice, yarn over and draw through all 3 loops on hook—1 st decreased.

NOTES
The Beret is worked in one piece in joined rnds from the top downwards. The RS will always be facing.

BERET
Beginning Ring
Wrap yarn around index finger. Insert hook into ring on finger, yarn over and draw up a loop. Carefully slip ring from finger and work the stitches of Rnd 1 into the ring.
Rnd 1 Ch 1, work 6 sc in ring; join with sl st in first sc.
Pull gently but firmly on tail to tighten center ring. In all following rnds work the first st(s) into the same sc as the joining sl st.
Rnd 2 Ch 1, 2 sc in each sc around; join with sl st in first sc—you will have 12 sc in this rnd.
Rnd 3 Ch 1, *sc in next sc, 2 sc in next sc; rep from * around; join with sl st in first sc—18 sc.
Rnd 4 Ch 1, sc in first sc, *2 sc in next sc, sc in next 2 sc; rep from * to last 2 sc, 2 sc in next sc, sc in last sc; join with sl st in first sc—24 sc.
Rnd 5 Ch 1, *sc in next 3 sc, 2 sc in next sc; rep from * around; join with sl st in first sc—30 sc.
Rnd 6 Ch 1, sc in first 2 sc, *2 sc in next sc, sc in next 4 sc; rep from * to last 3 sc, 2 sc in next sc, sc in last 2 sc; join with sl st in first sc—36 sc.
Rnd 7 Ch 1, *2 sc in next sc, sc in next 5 sc; rep from * around; join with sl st in first sc—42 sc.
Rnd 8 Ch 1, sc in first 3 sc, *2 sc in next sc, sc in next 6 sc; rep from * to last 4 sc, 2 sc in next sc, sc in last 3 sc; join with sl st in first sc—48 sc.
Rnd 9 Ch 1, *2 sc in next sc, sc in next 7 sc; rep from * around; join with sl st in first sc—54 sc.
Rnd 10 Ch 1, sc in first 6 sc, *2 sc in next sc, sc in next 8 sc; rep from * to last 3 sc, 2 sc in next sc, sc in last 2 sc; join with sl st in first sc—60 sc.
Rnd 11 Ch 1, sc in first 3 sc, *2 sc in next sc, sc in next 9 sc; rep from * to last 7 sc, 2 sc in next sc, sc in last 6 sc; join with sl st in first sc—66 sc.

Rnd 12 Ch 1, *2 sc in next sc, sc in next 10 sc; rep from * around; join with sl st in first sc—72 sc.

Rnd 13 Ch 1, sc in first 7 sc, *2 sc in next sc, sc in next 11 sc; rep from * to last 5 sc, 2 sc in next sc, sc in last 4 sc; join with sl st in first sc—78 sc.

Rnd 14 Ch 1, sc in first 3 sc, *2 sc in next sc, sc in next 12 sc; rep from * to last 10 sc, 2 sc in next sc, sc in last 9 sc; join with sl st in first sc—84 sc.

Rnd 15 Ch 1, sc in first 12 sc, *2 sc in next sc, sc in next 13 sc; rep from * to last 2 sc, 2 sc in next sc, sc in last sc; join with sl st in first sc—90 sc.

Rnd 16 Ch 1, sc in first 8 sc, *2 sc in next sc, sc in next 14 sc; rep from * to last 7 sc, 2 sc in next sc, sc in last 6 sc; join with sl st in first sc—96 sc.

Rnd 17 Ch 1, *2 sc in next sc, sc in next 15 sc; rep from * around; join with sl st in first sc—102 sc.

Rnd 18 Ch 1, sc in first 5 sc, *2 sc in next sc, sc in next 16 sc; rep from * to last 12 sc, 2 sc in next sc, sc in last 11 sc; join with sl st in first sc—108 sc.

Rnds 19–24 Ch 1, sc in each sc around; join with sl st in first sc.

Rnd 25 Ch 1, sc in first 6 sc, *sc2tog, sc in next 16 sc; rep from * to last 12 sc, sc2tog, sc in last 10 sc; join with sl st in first sc—102 sc.

Rnd 26 Ch 1, sc in each sc around; join with sl st in first sc.

Rnd 27 Ch 1, *sc2tog, sc in next 15 sc; rep from * around; join with sl st in first sc—96 sc.

Rnd 28 Ch 1, sc in each sc around; join with sl st in first sc.

Rnd 29 Ch 1, sc in first 8 sc, *sc2tog, sc in next 14 sc; rep from * to last 8 sc, sc2tog, sc in last 6 sc; join with sl st in first sc—90 sc.

Rnd 30 Ch 1, *sc2tog, sc in next 13 sc; rep from * around; join with sl st in first sc—84 sc.

Rnd 31 Ch 1, sc in first 4 sc, *sc2tog, sc in next 12 sc; rep from * to last 10 sc, sc2tog, sc in last 8 sc; join with sl st in first sc—78 sc.

Rnd 32 Ch 1, *sc2tog, sc in next 9 sc; rep from * to last 12 sc, sc2tog, sc in last 10 sc; join with sl st in first sc—71 sc.

Rnds 33–35 Working in back loops only, sc in each sc around; join wth sl st in first sc.

Rnd 36 Ch 1, working in back loops only, sl st in each sc around. Fasten off.

FINISHING

Weave in ends. •

Coney Island Frank Dog Toy

Easy

MEASUREMENTS
Approx 8"/20cm long

MATERIALS
Yarn
LION BRAND® Vanna's Choice®, 3½oz/100g balls, each 170yd/156m (acrylic, rayon)
- 1 ball in #123 Beige (A)
- 1 ball in #133 Brick (B)

Note Yarn amount is sufficient to make multiple Toys.

Hook
- Size G/6 (4mm) crochet hook, *or size needed to obtain gauge*

Notions
- Stitch markers
- Tapestry needle
- Small amount of fiberfill stuffing
- Small amount of mustard-colored yarn

GAUGE
EXACT GAUGE IS NOT ESSENTIAL FOR THIS PROJECT.

STITCH GLOSSARY
sc2tog (sc 2 sts together) (Insert hook in next st and draw up a loop) twice, yarn over and draw through all 3 loops on hook—1 st decreased.

NOTES
1) Frank and Bun are worked separately in continuous rnds; do not join or turn unless otherwise instructed.
2) A small hook and tight gauge for this yarn are used to create a dense fabric for the toy.

BUNS (Make 2)
With A, ch 2.
Rnd 1 Work 8 sc in first ch; place marker to indicate beg of rnd; move marker up as each rnd is completed.
Rnd 2 2 sc in each st around—you will have 16 sc at the end of this rnd.
Rnds 3–25 Sc in each st around. Stuff piece lightly.
Rnd 26 Sc2tog around—8 sc.
Fasten off and cut yarn, leaving a long yarn tail. Thread yarn tail into blunt needle and weave through last rnd. Pull gently to draw sts together and knot.

FRANK
With B, ch 2.
Rnd 1 Work 6 sc in first ch; place marker to indicate beg of rnd; move marker up as each rnd is completed.
Rnd 2 Work 2 sc in each st around—12 sc.
Rnds 3–17 Sc in each st around.
Begin to stuff piece firmly.
Rnds 18–32 Sc in each st around.
Finish stuffing piece.
Rnd 33 Sc2tog around—6 sc.
Fasten off and cut yarn, leaving a long yarn tail. Thread yarn tail into blunt needle and weave through last rnd. Pull gently to draw sts together and knot.

FINISHING
Sew Buns together along one long side.
With mustard yarn, embroider a chain st line of "mustard" onto Frank.
Sew Frank into Bun.
Weave in ends. •

Destin Beach Sun Hat

Easy

MEASUREMENTS
Circumference Approx 19½"/49.5cm, will stretch to fit a range of sizes
Height Approx 8½"/21.5cm

MATERIALS
Yarn
LION BRAND® 24/7 Cotton®, 3 1/2oz/100g balls; each 186yd/170m (cotton) (4)
• 1 ball in #158 Goldenrod

Hook
• Size H/8 (5mm) crochet hook, *or size needed to obtain gauge.*

Notions
• Stitch markers
• Tapestry needle

GAUGE
16 sc = Approx 4"/10cm using size H/8 (5mm) crochet hook.
TAKE TIME TO CHECK GAUGE.

NOTE
Hat is worked in one piece in continuous rnds.

HAT
Ch 2.
Work 6 sc in the first ch; join with sl st in first sc—6 sc.
Place marker for beginning of rnd and move marker up as each rnd is completed.
Rnd 1 Work 2 sc in each sc around — you will have 12 sc at the end of Rnd 1.
Rnd 2 *Work 2 sc in next sc, sc in next sc; rep from * around—18 sc.
Rnd 3 *Work 2 sc in next sc, sc in next 2 sc; rep from * around—24 sc.
Rnd 4 *Work 2 sc in next sc, sc in next 3 sc; rep from * around—30 sc.
Rnd 5 *Work 2 sc in next sc, sc in next 4 sc; rep from * around—36 sc.
Rnd 6 *Work 2 sc in next sc, sc in next 5 sc; rep from * around—42 sc.
Rnd 7 *Work 2 sc in next sc, sc in next 6 sc; rep from * around—48 sc.
Rnd 8 *Work 2 sc in next sc, sc in next 7 sc; rep from * around—54 sc.
Rnd 9 *Work 2 sc in next sc, sc in next 8 sc; rep from * around—60 sc.
Rnd 10 *Work 2 sc in next sc, sc in next 9 sc; rep from * around—66 sc.
Rnd 11 *Work 2 sc in the next sc, sc in next 10 sc* rep from * around—72 sc.
Rnd 12 *Work 2 sc in the next sc, sc in next 11 sc* rep from * around—78 sc.
Rnd 13 Working in back loops only, sc in each sc around.
Rnds 14–39 Sc in each sc around.
Rnd 40 *Work 2 sc in next sc, sc in next 2 sc; rep from * around—104 sc.
Rnds 41–45 Sc in each sc around.
Rnd 46 *Work 2 sc in next sc, sc in next 2 sc; rep from * to last 2 sc, sc in last 2 sc—138 sc.
Rnd 47 Sc in each sc around.
Join with sl st in first sc and fasten off.

FINISHING
Weave in ends. •

Trenton Tote

Easy

MEASUREMENTS
Circumference Approx 26"/66cm
Height (excluding handles) Approx 13½"/34.5cm

MATERIALS
Yarn
LION BRAND® 24/7 Cotton®, 3½oz/100g balls, each approx 186yd/170m (cotton) (4)
• 2 balls in #172 Grass

Hook
• One size I/9 (5.5mm) crochet hook, *or size needed to obtain gauge*

Notions
• Stitch markers
• Tapestry needle

GAUGE
EXACT GAUGE IS NOT ESSENTIAL TO THIS PROJECT.

NOTES
1) Base of Bag is worked in joined rnds with RS always facing. Do not turn at the beg of rnds of base.
2) Sides of Bag are worked in joined and turned rnds in a Diamond Lattice pattern. When working sides, turn at the beg of every rnd.
3) Top edge and straps are worked in a continuous spiral. Do join and do not turn at the beg of rnds.

TOTE
Base
Ch 3, join with sl st in first ch to form a ring.
Rnd 1 Ch 1, work 8 sc in ring; join with sl st in first sc—8 sc.
Rnd 2 Ch 1, work 2 sc in each st around; join with sl st in first sc—16 sc.
Rnd 3 Ch 1, (sc in next st, 2 sc in next st) 8 times; join with sl st in first sc—24 sc.
Rnd 4 Ch 1, (sc in next 2 sts, 2 sc in next st) 8 times; join with sl st in first sc—32 sc.
Rnd 5 Ch 1, (sc in next 3 sts, 2 sc in next st) 8 times; join with sl st in first sc—40 sc.
Rnd 6 Ch 1, (sc in next 4 sts, 2 sc in next st) 8 times; join with sl st in first sc—48 sc.
Rnd 7 Ch 1, (sc in next 5 sts, 2 sc in next st) 8 times; join with sl st in first sc—56 sc.
Rnd 8 Ch 1, (sc in next 6 sts, 2 sc in next st) 8 times; join with sl st in first sc—64 sc.
Rnd 9 Ch 1, (sc in next 7 sts, 2 sc in next st) 8 times; join with sl st in first sc—72 sc.
Rnd 10 Ch 1, (sc in next 8 sts, 2 sc in next st) 8 times; join with sl st in first sc—80 sc.
Rnd 11 Ch 1, (sc in next 9 sts, 2 sc in next st) 8 times; join with sl st in first sc—88 sc.
Rnd 12 Ch 1, (sc next 10 sts, 2 sc in next st) 8 times; join with sl st in first sc—96 sc.
Rnd 13 Ch 1, (sc in next 11 sts, 2 sc in next st) 8 times; join with sl st in first sc—104 sc.

Begin Diamond Lattice Pattern
Rnd 1 (RS) Ch 1, sc in next 2 sts, *ch 5, skip next 3 sts, sc in next 5 sts; rep from * to last 6 sts, ch 5, skip next 3 sts, sc in last 3 sts; join with sl st in first sc—you will have 65 sc and 13 ch-5 sps in this rnd.
Rnd 2 (WS) Ch 1, turn, sc in first 2 sc, ch 3, sc in next ch-5 sp, *ch 3, sk next sc, sc in next 3 sc, ch 3, sc in next ch-5 sp; rep from * to last 2 sc, ch 3, sc in last 2 sc; join with sl st in first sc—53 sc and 26 ch-3 sps.
Rnd 3 Ch 1, turn, sc in first sc, *ch 3, sc in next ch-3 sp, sc in next sc, sc in next ch-3 sp, ch 3, sk next sc, sc in next sc; rep from * around; join with sl st in first sc—53 sc and 26 ch-3 sps.
Rnd 4 Ch 7 (counts as tr, ch 3), turn, sc in next ch-3 sp, sc in next 3 sc, sc in next ch-3 sp, *ch 5, sc in next ch-3 sp, sc in next 3 sc, sc in next ch-3 sp; rep from * to last sc, ch 3, tr in last sc; join with sl st in 4th ch of beg ch-7—2 tr, 65 sc, 2 ch-3 sps and 12 ch-5 sps.
Rnd 5 Ch 1, turn, sc in first tr, ch 3, sk first ch-3 sp, sk next sc, sc in next 3 sc, *ch 3, sc in next ch-5 sp, ch 3, sk next sc, sc in next 3 sc; rep from * to last ch-sp, ch 3, sc in same ch as joining; join with sl st in first sc—53 sc and 26 ch-3 sps.
Rnd 6 Ch 1, turn, sc in first sc, sc next in ch-3 sp, ch 3, sk next sc, sc in next sc, *ch 3, sc in next ch-3 sp, sc in next sc, sc in next ch-3 sp, ch 3, sk next sc, sc in next sc; rep from * to last ch-3 sp, ch 3, sc in last ch-3 sp, sc in last sc; join with sl st in first sc—53 sc and 26 ch-3 sps.
Rnd 7 (RS) Ch 1, turn, sc in first 2 sc, sc in next ch-3 sp, ch 5, sc in

Trenton Tote

next ch-3 sp, *sc in next 3 sc, sc in next ch-3 sp, ch 5, sc in next ch-3 sp; rep from * to last 2 sc, sc in last 2 sc; join with sl st in first sc—65 sc and 13 ch-5 sps.

Rep Rnds 2–7 until piece measures approx 10"/25.5cm from last rnd of base, end with a Rnd 7 as the last rnd you work.

Top Edge and Straps
Rnd 1 (RS) Ch 1, work 84 sc evenly spaced around top edge of Bag; do not join with a sl st, work in a continuous spiral—84 sts. Place marker for beg of rnd, move marker up as each rnd is completed.
Rnds 2–4 Sc in each sc around.
Rnd 5 Sc in next 15 sts, ch 50 for strap, sk next 12 sts, sc in next 30 sts, ch 50 for strap, sk next 12 sts, sc in last 15 sts.
Rnd 6 Sc in each sc and ch around—160 sc.
Rnds 7–9 Sc in each sc around.
Fasten off.

FINISHING
Weave in ends.•

Tenafly Scarf

Basic

MEASUREMENTS
Approx 7"/18cm wide x 58"/147.5cm long

MATERIALS
Yarn
LION BRAND® Mandala®, Thick & Quick® 5.3oz/150g balls; each 87yd/79m (acrylic) 🔟
- 2 balls in #209 Thumbprint

Hook
- Size N (10mm) crochet hook, *or size needed to obtain gauge*

Notions
- Tapestry needle

GAUGE
7 hdc and 6 rows = 4"/10cm using size N (10mm) hook. *TAKE TIME TO CHECK GAUGE.*

NOTES
1) Scarf is worked in one piece lengthwise.
2) Hdc sts are worked in back loops to create a textured look.

SCARF
Ch 101.
Row 1 Sc in 2nd ch from hook and in each ch across—100 sc.
Row 2 Ch 2 (counts as first hdc), turn, working in back loops only, hdc in next st and in each st to last st; working in both loops, hdc in last st.
Rows 3–10 Ch 2 (counts as first hdc), turn, working in back loops only, hdc in next st and in each st to last st; hdc in top of beg ch.
Row 11 Ch 1, turn, sc in first st and in each st to last st; sc in top of beg ch.
Fasten off.

FINISHING
Weave in ends. •

One-Ball Bobble Cowl

Easy

MEASUREMENTS
Circumference Approx 24"/61cm
Height Approx 11½"/29cm

MATERIALS
Yarn
LION BRAND® Scarfie®, 5.3oz/150g balls; each 312yd/285m (acrylic, wool) [5]
• 1 ball in #213 Black/Hot Pink

Hook
• Size K/10½ (6.5mm) crochet hook, *or size needed to obtain gauge.*

Notions
• Tapestry needle

GAUGE
10½ sc = 4"/10cm using size K/10½ (6.5mm). *TAKE TIME TO CHECK GAUGE.*

STITCH GLOSSARY
Bobble Yarn over, insert hook in indicated st and draw up a loop, yarn over and draw through 2 loops on hook (2 loops rem on hook), (yarn over, insert hook in same st and draw up a loop, yarn over and draw through 2 loops on hook) 3 times (5 loops rem on hook), yarn over, draw through all loops on hook.
Note Bobbles are worked on WS of the Cowl. When you finish making the Cowl, gently push each Bobble to the RS of work.

NOTES
1) Cowl is worked in one piece in joined rnds.
2) The beginning and ending borders of the Cowl are worked on the RS; all the rnds in the Bobbles section of the Cowl are worked on the WS.
3) If you find it difficult to join the beg ch into a ring without twisting the ch, Rnd 1 can be worked as a row, then joined into a rnd, as follows: Leaving a long beg tail, ch 66, hdc in 3rd ch from hook (2 skipped ch do not count as a st) and in each ch across; join with sl st in top of beg ch—you will have 64 hdc at the end of this row/rnd. Use beg tail to sew gap at base of row closed. Proceed to Rnd 2.

COWL
Ch 65; taking care not to twist ch, join with sl st in first ch to form a ring.

Border
Note All rnds of the border are worked on the RS, so do NOT turn your work.
Rnd 1 (RS) Ch 2 (does not count as a st), hdc in next ch and in each ch around; join with sl st in top of beg ch—you will have 64 hdc.
Rnds 2 and 3 Ch 2 (does not count as a st), hdc each st around; join with sl st in top of beg ch.

Bobbles
Note When you turn your work at the beginning of the Set-up Rnd, you will be working on the WS. You'll continue to work only on the WS (NOT turning) until all the rnds of the Bobble section of the Cowl are complete.
Set-up Rnd (WS) Ch 1, TURN, sc in each st around; join with sl st in beg ch—64 sc.
Rnd 1 Ch 3 (does not count as a st), do NOT turn, Bobble in first st, dc in next st, *Bobble in next st, dc in next st; rep from * around; join with sl st in top of beg ch—32 Bobbles and 32 dc.
Rnd 2 Ch 1, sc in each st around; join with sl st in beg ch—64 sc.
Rnd 3 Ch 3 (does not count as a st), dc in first st, Bobble in next st, *dc in next st, Bobble in next st; rep from * around; join with sl st in top of beg ch.
Rnd 4 Rep Rnd 2.
Rep Rnds 1–4 until piece measures about 10½"/26.5cm from beg, end with a Rnd 2 or Rnd 4 as the last rnd you work.

Border
Note When you turn your work at the beginning of border Rnd 1, you will be working on the RS. Do NOT turn when you work Rnds 2

and 3 of the border.

Rnd 1 (RS) Ch 2 (does not count as a st), TURN, hdc in each st around; join with sl st in top of beg ch.

Rnds 2 and 3 Ch 2 (does not count as a st), do NOT turn, hdc in each st around; join with sl st in top of beg ch. Fasten off.

FINISHING

Weave in ends. •

Kent Street Bagel Cat Toy

Easy

MEASUREMENTS
Approx 4"/10cm in diameter

MATERIALS
Yarn
LION BRAND® Vanna's Choice®, 3½oz/100g balls; each 170yd/156m (acrylic, rayon) [4]
• 1 ball in #123 Beige
Note Yarn amount is sufficient to make multiple Toys.

Hook
• Size G/6 (4mm) crochet hook, *or size needed to obtain gauge*

Notions
• Stitch markers
• Tapestry needle
• Small amount of fiberfill stuffing
• Small amount of catnip

GAUGE
EXACT GAUGE IS NOT ESSENTIAL FOR THIS PROJECT.

STITCH GLOSSARY
sc2tog (sc 2 sts together) (Insert hook in next st and draw up a loop) twice, yarn over and draw through all 3 loops on hook—1 st decreased.

NOTES
1) Bagel is worked in continuous rnds; do not join or turn unless otherwise instructed.
2) We used a smaller hook than usual for this yarn to create a dense fabric for this toy.

BAGEL
Ch 12; join with sl st in first ch to form a ring.
Rnd 1 Work *2 sc in first ch, sc in next ch; rep from * around—you will have 18 sc at the end of this rnd. Pm to indicate beg of rnd; move marker up as each rnd is completed.
Rnd 2 Sc in each st around.
Rnd 3 Work *2 sc in next st, sc in next 2 sts; rep from * around—24 sc.
Rnd 4 Sc in each st around.
Rnd 5 Work *2 sc in next st, sc in next 3 sts; rep from * around—30 sc.
Rnd 6 Work *2 sc in next st, sc in next 2 sts; rep from * around—40 sc.
Rnd 7 Work *2 sc in next st, sc in next 3 sts; rep from * around—50 sc.
Rnds 8–12 Sc in each st around.
Rnd 13 *Sc2tog, sc in each of next 3 sts; rep from * around—40 sc.
Rnd 14 *Sc2tog, sc in each of next 2 sts; rep from * around—30 sc.
Rnd 15 *Sc2tog, sc in each of next 3 sts; rep from * around—24 sc.
Rnd 16 Sc in each st around.
Rnd 17 *Sc2tog, sc in each of next 2 sts; rep from * around—18 sc.
Rnd 18 Sc in each st around.
Rnd 19 *Sc2tog, sc in next st; rep from * around—12 sc.
Rnd 20 Sc in each st around.
Fasten off.

FINISHING
Stuff piece firmly with fiberfill and catnip.
Sew first rnd to last to make Bagel.
Weave in ends. •

Peabody Hat and Mitts

Basic

MEASUREMENTS
Hat
Circumference Approx 19"/48.5cm; will stretch to fit a range of sizes
Height Approx 9"/23cm

Mitts
Circumference Approx 9"/23cm; will stretch to fit a range of sizes
Height Approx 9"/23cm

MATERIALS
Yarn
LION BRAND® Landscapes®, 3½oz/100g balls; each 147yd/134m (acrylic)
• 2 balls in #206 Metropolis

Hook
• Size J/10 (6mm) crochet hook, *or size needed to obtain gauge*

Notions
• Tapestry needle

GAUGE
12 hdc = 4"/10cm using size J/10 (6mm) hook. *TAKE TIME TO CHECK GAUGE.*

NOTES
1) Both Hat and Mitts are each made in 2 halves.
2) The halves are sewn together following diagrams.

HAT
Halves (make 2)
Ch 30.
Row 1 Hdc in 3rd ch from hook (2 skipped ch do not count as a st), and in each ch across—you will have 28 hdc.
Row 2 Ch 2 (does not count as a stitch), turn, hdc in each st across.

Rows 3–22 Rep Row 2.
Fasten off.

FINISHING

Following diagram, sew sides of Halves together along one side, then sew remaining sides together to make a tube.
Thread yarn into blunt needle and weave in and out of sts around one open end of tube.
Pull yarn to gather, then knot for top of Hat.

MITTS

First Half (make 2)
Ch 30.
Row 1 Rep Row 1 of Hat.
Rows 2–9 Rep Row 2 of Hat.
Fasten off.

Second Half (make 2)
Ch 14.
Row 1 Hdc in 3rd ch from hook (2 skipped ch do not count as a st), and in each ch across—you will have 12 hdc.
Rows 2–22 Rep Row 2 of Hat.
Fasten off.

FINISHING

Following diagram, sew sides of First and Second Halves together along one side.
Sew remaining sides together, leaving an opening for thumb.
Weave in ends. •

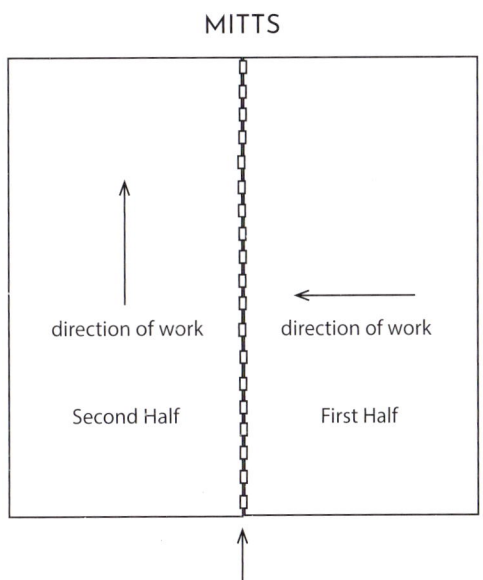

MITTS

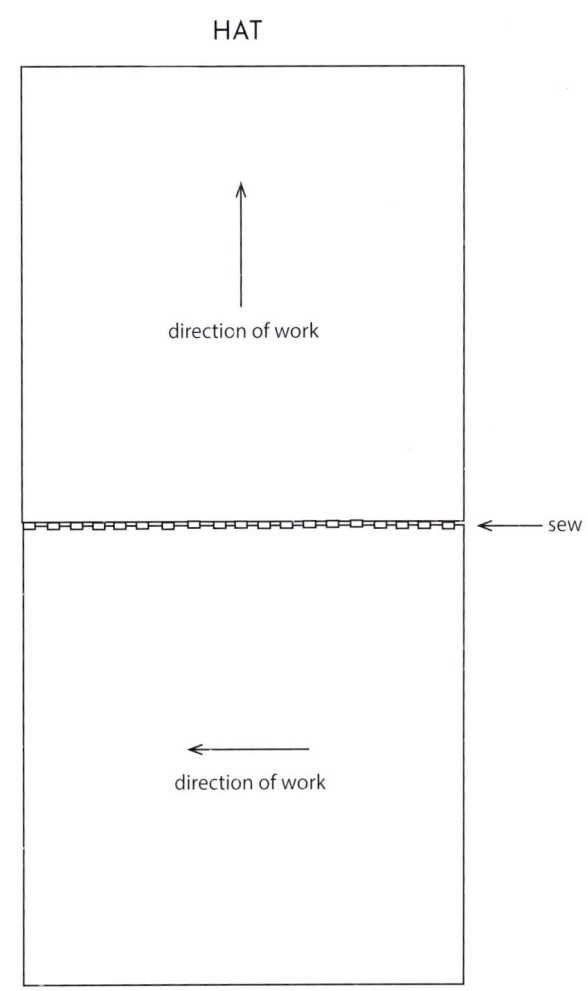

HAT

Lila Bobble Cowl

Easy

MEASUREMENTS
Circumference Approx 24"/61cm
Height Approx 11½"/29cm

MATERIALS
Yarn
LION BRAND® Vel-Luxe®, 5.3oz/150g balls; each 246yd/225m (polyester)
• 1 ball in #144 Lilac

Hook
• Size K/10½ (6.5mm) crochet hook, *or size needed to obtain gauge.*

Notions
• Tapestry needle

GAUGE
10½ sc = 4"/10cm using size K/10½ (6.5mm) hook.
TAKE TIME TO CHECK GAUGE.

STITCH GLOSSARY
Bobble Yarn over, insert hook in indicated st and draw up a loop, yarn over and draw through 2 loops on hook (2 loops rem on hook), (yarn over, insert hook in same st and draw up a loop, yarn over and draw through 2 loops on hook) 3 times (5 loops rem on hook), yarn over, draw through all loops on hook.
Note Bobbles are worked on the WS of the Cowl. When you finish making the Cowl, gently push each Bobble to the RS of work.

NOTES
1) Cowl is worked in one piece in joined rnds.
2) The borders of the Cowl are worked on the RS; all the rnds in the Bobbles section of the Cowl are worked on the WS.
3) If you find it difficult to join the beg ch into a ring without twisting the ch, Rnd 1 can be worked as a row, then joined into a rnd, as follows: Leaving a long beg tail, ch 66, hdc in 3rd ch from hook (2 skipped ch do not count as a st) and in each ch across; join with sl st in top of beg ch—you will have 64 hdc at the end of this row/rnd. Use beg tail to sew gap at base of row closed. Proceed to Rnd 2.

COWL
Ch 65; taking care not to twist ch, join with sl st in first ch to form a ring.
Note All rnds of the border are worked on the RS, so do *not* turn your work.

Border
Rnd 1 (RS) Ch 2 (does not count as a st), hdc in next ch and in each ch around; join with sl st in top of beg ch—you will have 64 hdc.
Rnds 2 and 3 Ch 2 (does not count as a st), hdc each st around; join with sl st in top of beg ch.

Bobbles
Note When you turn your work at the beginning of the Set-up Rnd, you'll be working on the WS. You'll continue to work only on the WS (*not* turning) until all the rnds of the Bobble section of the Cowl are complete.
Set-up Rnd (WS) Ch 1, *turn*, sc in each st around; join with sl st in beg ch—64 sc.
Rnd 1 Ch 3 (does not count as a st), do NOT turn, *Bobble in next st, dc in next st; rep from * around; join with sl st in top of beg ch—32 Bobbles and 32 dc.

Rnd 2 Ch 1, sc in each st around; join with sl st in beg ch—64 sc.
Rnd 3 Ch 3 (does not count as a st), *dc in next st, Bobble in next st; rep from * around; join with sl st in top of beg ch.
Rnd 4 Rep Rnd 2.
Rep Rnds 1–4 until piece measures about 10½"/26.5cm from beg, end with a Rnd 2 or Rnd 4 as the last rnd you work.

Border
Note When you turn your work at the beginning of border Rnd 1, you will be working on the RS. Do NOT turn when you work Rnds 2 and 3 of the border.

Rnd 1 (RS) Ch 2 (does not count as a st), *turn*, hdc in each st around; join with sl st in top of beg ch.
Rnds 2 and 3 Ch 2 (does not count as a st), do *not* turn, hdc in each st around; join with sl st in top of beg ch.
Fasten off.

FINISHING
Weave in ends. •

Pop of Color Garland

Easy

MEASUREMENTS
Approx 30"/76cm long, or length as desired

MATERIALS
Yarn
LION BRAND® Bonbons®, 2.8oz/80g packages; each 224yd/208m (acrylic)
- 2 packages in #610 Brights (A)
- 1 package in #620 Pastels (B)

Note Yarn is sold in packages of 8 miniature balls of yarn.

Hook
- Size H/8 (5mm) crochet hook, *or size needed to obtain gauge.*

Notions
- Tapestry needle

GAUGE
EXACT GAUGE IS NOT ESSENTIAL FOR THIS PROJECT.

NOTES
1) 56 Squares are worked individually, then strung onto crocheted chains to make the Garland.
2) When instructed to work with A or B, use any color of your choice from the indicated package of Bonbons. All pieces are made with 2 strands of yarn held tog. You can use 2 strands of the same color or one strand each of 2 different colors, whichever you like!

LARGE SQUARE (Make 8)
With 2 strands of any color of A held tog, ch 4; join with sl st in first ch to form a ring.
Rnd 1 Ch 5 (counts as dc, ch 2), (3 dc in ring, ch 2) 3 times, 2 dc in ring; join with sl st in 3rd ch of beg ch—at the end of Rnd 1 you will have 4 ch-2 sps and 12 dc.
Rnd 2 Sl st in first ch-sp, ch 5 (counts as dc, ch 2), 2 dc in same ch-sp, *dc in each dc to next ch-2 sp, (2 dc, ch 2, 2 dc) in ch-2 sp; rep from * 2 more times, dc in each dc to first ch-sp, dc in first ch-sp; join with sl st in 3rd ch of beg ch—4 ch-2 sps and 28 dc (7 dc across each of 4 sides).
Rnd 3 Rep Rnd 2—4 ch-2 sps and 44 dc (11 dc across each of 4 sides).
Fasten off.

ONE-COLOR MEDIUM SQUARES (Make 18)
Note Make 6 Squares with 2 strands of A held tog, 6 Squares with 2 strands of B held tog, and 6 Squares with 1 strand each of A and B held tog.
Ch 4; join with sl st in first ch to form a ring.
Rnds 1 and 2 Work same as Rnds 1 and 2 of Large Square.
Fasten off.

TWO-COLOR MEDIUM SQUARES (Make 6)
With 2 strands of A held tog, ch 4; join with sl st in first ch to form a ring.
Rnd 1 Work same as Rnd 1 of Large Square.
Fasten off.
Rnd 2 From RS, join 2 strands of B with sl st in first ch-sp, ch 5 (counts as dc, ch 2), 2 dc in same ch-sp, *dc in each dc to next ch-2 sp, (2 dc, ch 2, 2 dc) in ch-2 sp; rep from * 2 more times, dc in each dc to first ch-sp, dc in first ch-sp; join with sl st in 3rd ch of beg ch—4 ch-2 sps and 28 dc (7 dc across each of 4 sides).
Fasten off.

SMALL SQUARES (Make 24)
Note Make 6 Squares with 2 strands of A held tog, 6 Squares with 2 strands of B held tog, and 12 Squares with 1 strand each of A and B held tog.
Ch 4; join with sl st in first ch to form a ring.
Rnd 1 Work same as Rnd 1 of Large Square.
Fasten off.

GARLANDS (Make 4)
Note Make each Garland with 2 strands of any of the yarns held tog.
Ch 12; join with sl st in first ch to make the first hanging loop, then chain until piece measures about 33"/84cm from beg, then sl st in 13th ch from hook.
Fasten off.

FINISHING

Make a pile of 14 Squares arranged (from bottom to top of the pile) in the following order:
Large Square
(Small Square, Medium Square) 3 times
Large Square
(Small Square, Medium Square) 3 times

String Squares onto the Garland by working from the top to bottom of the pile as follows:
Weave Garland in and out of ch-2 sps diagonally across each Square.
Rep with remaining Garlands and Squares.
Weave in ends. •

Hooded Scarf with Pockets

Basic

MEASUREMENTS
Scarf Approx 8"/20.5cm x 74"/188cm
Hood Approx 10"/25.5cm x 16"/40.5cm

MATERIALS
Yarn
LION BRAND® Go for Faux Thick & Quick®, Bonus Bundle, 10½oz/300g balls; each 59yd/54m (polyester)
• 4 balls in #200 Mink

Hook
• Size S/35 (19mm) crochet hook, *or size needed to obtain gauge.*

Notions
• Tapestry needle

GAUGE
4 sc = 4"/10cm using size S/35 (19mm) hook. *TAKE TIME TO CHECK GAUGE.*

NOTES
1) Scarf is worked in one piece. Ends of Scarf are folded and seamed to create pockets.
2) Hood is worked separately, then sewn to Scarf.

SCARF
Ch 9.
Row 1 Sc in 2nd ch from hook and each ch across—you'll have 8 sc.
Row 2 Ch 1, turn, sc in each sc across.
Rep Row 2 until piece measures about 74"/188cm from beginning. Fasten off and cut yarn, leaving a long tail for sewing.

HOOD

Ch 11.

Row 1 Sc in 2nd ch from hook and each ch across—you'll have 10 sc.

Row 2 Ch 1, turn, sc in each sc across.

Rep Row 2 until piece measures about 16"/40.5cm.

Fasten off and cut yarn, leaving a long tail for sewing.

FINISHING

Pockets

Following diagram, fold each end of Scarf back about 8½"/21.5cm. Sew sides of each pocket.

Hood

Fold hood in half to make an 8"/20.5cm x 10"/25.5cm piece.

Seam one end for top of hood.

Match center of hood to center of Scarf, then sew hood to Scarf. Weave in ends. •

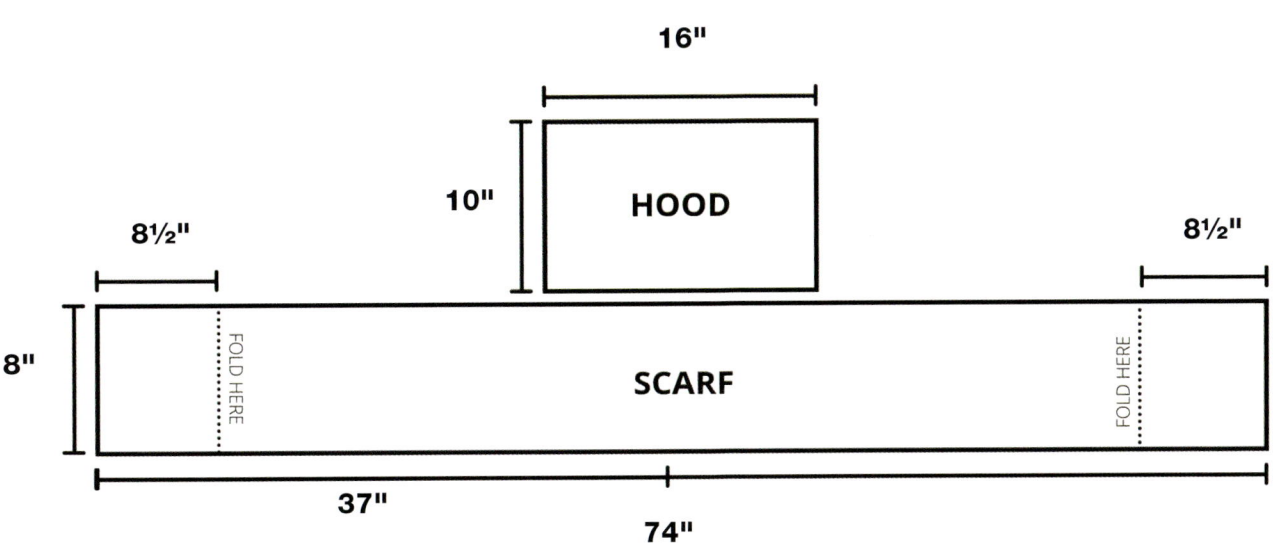

The Poet Dog Sweater

Easy

SIZES
S (M/L, 1X/2X)
Note Pattern is written for smallest size with changes for larger sizes in parentheses. When only one number is given, it applies to all sizes.

MEASUREMENTS
Neck Circumference 11 (13 1/2, 16)"/28 (34.5, 40.5)cm
Chest 18½ (22 1/2, 26)"/47 (57, 66)cm
Length 14 (18, 22)"/(35.5 45.5, 56)cm

MATERIALS
Yarn
LION BRAND® Homespun®, 6oz/170g balls; each 185yd/169m (acrylic, polyester)
- 2 (2, 3) skeins in #312 Edwardian

Hook
- Size K/10½ (6.5mm) crochet hook, *or size needed to obtain gauge*

Notions
- Tapestry needle

GAUGE
10 sc and 10 rows = 4"/10cm using size K/10½ (6.5mm) hook. *TAKE TIME TO CHECK GAUGE.*

STITCH GLOSSARY
BPDC (back post double crochet) Yarn over, insert hook from back to front then to back, going around post of indicated st, draw up a loop, (yarn over and draw through 2 loops on hook) twice. Skip st in front of the BPDC.
FPDC (front post double crochet) Yarn over, insert hook from front to back then to front, going around post of indicated st, draw up a loop, (yarn over and draw through 2 loops on hook) twice. Skip st behind the FPDC.
sc2tog (sc 2 sts together) (Insert hook in next st and draw up a loop) twice, yarn over and draw through all 3 loops on hook—1 st decreased.

NOTES
1) Sweater is made in 2 pieces: Back and Underpiece.
2) Pieces are worked separately and then sewn together, leaving openings for legs.

BACK
Ch 33 (41, 49).
Row 1 (RS) Sc in 2nd ch from hook and in each ch across—32 (40, 48) sc.
Row 2 Ch 1, turn, sc in each st across.
Rep Row 2 until piece measures approx 9 (12½, 15½)"/23 (32, 39.5)cm from beg.

Shape Top
Decrease Row Ch 1, turn, sc2tog, sc in each st to last 3 sts, sc2tog, sc in last st—30 (38, 46) sts.
Next Row Ch 1, turn, sc in each st across.
Rep last 2 rows until—20 (26, 32) sts rem.
Fasten off.

UNDERPIECE
Ch 15 (17, 19).
Row 1 (RS) Sc in 2nd ch from hook and in each ch across—14 (16, 18) sc.
Row 2 Ch 1, turn, sc in each st across.
Rep Row 2 until piece measures about 4 (7, 10)"/10 (18, 25.5)cm from beg.

Shape Top
Decrease Row Ch 1, turn, sc2tog, sc in each st to last 3 sts, sc2tog, sc in last st—12 (14, 16) sts.
Next Row Ch 1, turn, sc in each st across.
Rep last 2 rows until—8 sts rem.
Fasten off.

The Poet Dog Sweater

FINISHING

Beg at neck edge, sew sides of Underpiece to Back for 1½ (2, 2½)"/4 (5, 6.5)cm; leave next 1½ (2, 2½)"/4 (5, 6.5)cm open for legs, then sew remainder of Underpiece to Back. Note that the lower portion of the Back remains unsewn.

Neck Trim

Rnd 1 (RS) From RS, join yarn with sc in any st along neck edge, work 31 (39, 45) more sc evenly spaced around neck edge; join with sl st in first sc—32 (40, 46) sc.
Rnd 2 Ch 2 (does not count as a st), FPDC around same sc as joining, BPDC around next st, *FPDC around next st, BPDC around next st; rep from * around; join with sl st in top of beg ch.
Rnds 3–5 Ch 2, *FPDC around next FPDC, BPDC around next BPDC; rep from * around; join with sl st in top of beg ch.
Fasten off.

Leg Opening Trim

Rnd 1 (RS) From RS, join yarn with sc anywhere along edge of leg opening, work 15 (19, 25) more sc evenly spaced around edge of leg opening; join with sl st in first sc—16 (20, 26) sc.
Rnd 2 Rep Rnd 2 of Neck Trim.
Fasten off.
Rep on opposite leg opening.

Lower Edge Trim

From RS, join yarn with sc anywhere along lower edge of Sweater, work sc evenly spaced around lower edge, working 2 sc in each corner; join with sl st in first sc.
Fasten off.
Weave in ends. •

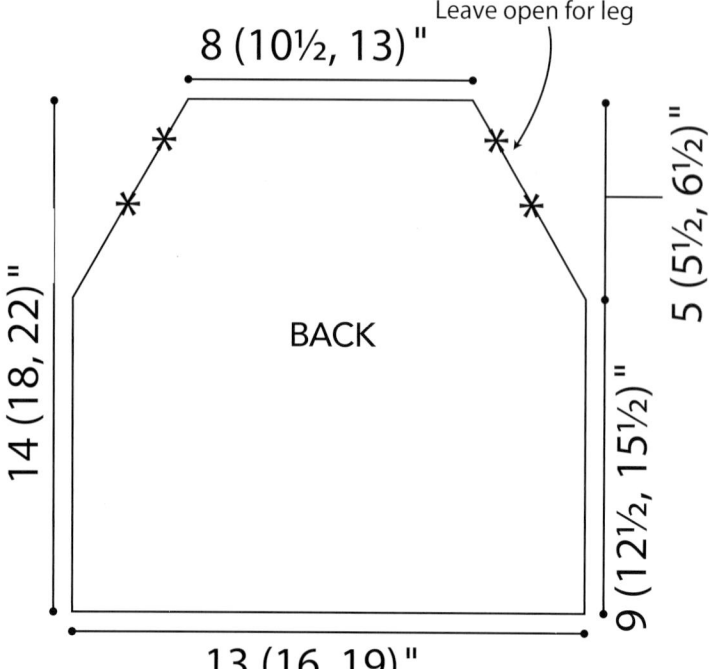
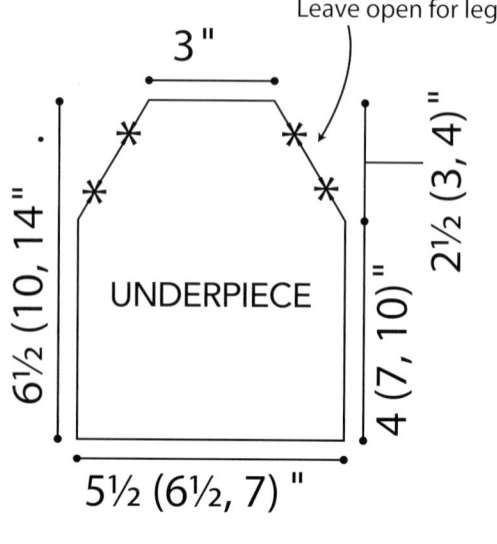

Crochet Soap Sack

Basic

MEASUREMENTS
Approx 4"/10cm x 6"/15cm

MATERIALS
Yarn
LION BRAND® 24/7 Cotton®, 3½oz/100g balls; each 186yd/170m (cotton)
• 1 ball in #101 Pink or any desired color
Note One ball of yarn will make 2–3 Sacks.

Hook
• Size G/6 (4mm) crochet hook, *or size needed to obtain gauge*

Notions
• Tapestry needle

GAUGE
EXACT GAUGE IS NOT IMPORTANT FOR THIS PROJECT.

NOTE
Sack is worked in one piece.

SACK
Make a slip knot on your hook and ch 5.
Join the last ch to the first with a slip st to make a ring.
Rnd 1 Ch 1, work 12 dc in ring; slip st in beg ch to join.
Rnd 2 (Increase Rnd) Ch 2, *work 2 dc in next st, dc in next st; rep from * around, slip st in beg chain to join. You'll have 18 dc.
Rnd 3 (Increase Rnd) Rep Rnd 2—27 dc.
Rnd 4 Ch 2, dc in each st around, join with slip st in beg ch.
Rnds 5–10 Rep Rnd 4.
Last Rnd and Loop Ch 1, sc in each st around, join with slip st in beg ch; then chain 14, slip st in edge of Sack near last join. Fasten off.

FINISHING
Weave in yarn ends. •

Fenwick Scarf

Easy

MEASUREMENTS
Approx 19 x 70" (48.5 x 178 cm)

MATERIALS
Yarn
LION BRAND® Homespun®, New Look, 6oz/170g balls; each 185yd/169m (acrylic)
• 4 balls in #601 First Blush

Hook
• Size K/10½ (6.5mm) crochet hook, *or size needed to obtain gauge.*

Notions
• Tapestry needle

GAUGE
1 pattern rep = about 2½"/6.5cm using size K/10½ (6.5mm).
Note One pattern rep consists of sc (ch 9, sl st) twice, sc and the following ch-4 sp. *TAKE TIME TO CHECK GAUGE.*

NOTES
1) Scarf is worked in one piece.
2) For those who find a visual helpful, we've included a stitch diagram.

SCARF
Ch 57.
Row 1 Sc in 2nd ch from hook, ch 9, sl st in last sc made, sc in next ch, *ch 4, sk next 4 ch, sc in next ch, (ch 9, sl st in last sc made) twice, sc in next ch; rep from * to last 6 ch, ch 4, sk next 4 ch, sc in next ch, ch 9, sl st in last sc made, sc in last ch—you will have 20 sc, 9 ch-4 sps, and 18 ch-9 sps in this row (for 9 pattern reps).
Row 2 Ch 6 (counts as tr, ch 2), turn, (sc in 5th ch of next ch-9 sp) twice, *ch 4, (sc in 5th ch of next ch-9 sp) twice; rep from * across, ch 2, tr in last sc—2 tr, 18 sc, 8 ch-4 sps, and 2 ch-2 sps.
Row 3 Ch 1, turn, sc in first st, ch 2, sk first ch-2 sp, sc in next sc, (ch 9, sl st in last sc made) twice, sc in next sc, *ch 4, sk next ch-4 sp, sc in next sc, (ch 9, sl st in last sc made) twice, sc in next sc; rep from * to beg ch, ch 2, sc in 4th ch of beg ch-6—20 sc, 2 ch-2 sps, 8 ch-4 sps, and 18 ch-9 sps.
Row 4 Ch 4 (counts as tr), turn, sc in 5th ch of first ch-9 sp, *ch 4, (sc in 5th ch of next ch-9 sp) twice; rep from * to last ch-9 sp, ch 4, sc in 5th ch of last ch-9 sp, tr in last sc—2 tr, 18 sc, and 9 ch-4 sps.
Row 5 Ch 1, turn, sc in first st, ch 9, sl st in last sc made, sc in next st, *ch 4, sk next ch-4 sp, sc in next sc, (ch 9, sl st in last sc made) twice, sc in next sc; rep from * to last ch-4 sp, ch 4, sk last ch-4 sp, sc in next sc, ch 9, sl st in last sc made, sc in top of beg ch-4—20 sc, 9 ch-4 sps, and 18 ch-9 sps.
Rep Rows 2–5 until piece measures about 70"/178cm from beg, end with a Row 4 as the last row you work.
Last Row Ch 1, turn, sc in first 2 sts, *ch 4, sk next ch-4 sp, sc in next 2 sc; rep from * to last ch-4 sp, ch 4, sk last ch-4 sp, sc in next sc, sc in top of beg ch-4—20 sc and 9 ch-4 sps.
Fasten off.

FINISHING
Weave in ends. •

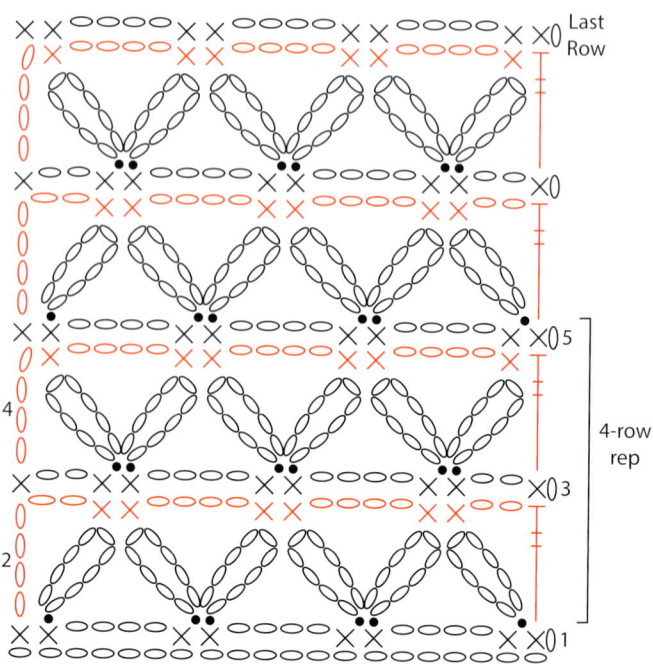

Heige Hat

Easy

MEASUREMENTS
Circumference Approx 20"/51cm, will stretch to fit a range of sizes
Height Approx 8"/20.5cm

MATERIALS
Yarn
LION BRAND® Scarfie®, 5.3oz/150g balls; each 312yd/285m (acrylic, wool)
• 1 ball in #206 Cream/Taupe

Hook
• Size K/10½ (6.5mm) crochet hook, *or size needed to obtain gauge.*

Notions
• Tapestry needle

GAUGE
11 hdc = 4"/10cm using size K/10½ (6.5mm) hook. *TAKE TIME TO CHECK GAUGE.*

STITCH GLOSSARY
Bobble Yarn over, insert hook in indicated st and draw up a loop, yarn over and draw through 2 loops on hook (2 loops rem on hook), (yarn over, insert hook in same st and draw up a loop, yarn over and draw through 2 loops on hook) 3 times (5 loops rem on hook), yarn over, draw through all loops on hook.
hdc2tog (hdc 2 sts together) (Yarn over, insert hook in next st and draw up a loop) twice, yarn over and draw through all 5 loops on hook—1 st decreased.

NOTES
1) Hat is worked in one piece in joined rnds, beginning at top of Hat.
2) All rnds in Bobble band are worked on WS. This becomes the RS when the band is folded up.

HAT
Ch 3.
Rnd 1 (RS) Work 8 hdc in 3rd ch from hook (2 skipped ch do not count as a st); join with sl st in first hdc—you will have 8 hdc.
Rnd 2 Ch 2 (does not count as a st), 2 hdc in each st around; join with sl st in first hdc—you will have 16 hdc at the end of this rnd.
Rnd 3 Ch 2 (does not count as a st), hdc in first st, 2 hdc in next st, *hdc in next st, 2 hdc in next st; rep from * around; join with sl st in first hdc—24 hdc.
Rnd 4 Ch 2 (does not count as a st), hdc in first 2 sts, 2 hdc in next st, *hdc in next 2 sts, 2 hdc in next st; rep from * around; join with sl st in first hdc—32 hdc.
Rnd 5 Ch 2 (does not count as a st), hdc in first 3 sts, 2 hdc in next st, *hdc in next 3 sts, 2 hdc in next st; rep from * around; join with sl st in first hdc—40 hdc.
Rnd 6 Ch 2 (does not count as a st), hdc in first 4 sts, 2 hdc in next st, *hdc in next 4 sts, 2 hdc in next st; rep from * around; join with sl st in first hdc—48 hdc.
Rnd 7 Ch 2 (does not count as a st), hdc in first 5 sts, 2 hdc in next st, *hdc in next 5 sts, 2 hdc in next st; rep from * around; join with sl st in first hdc—56 hdc.
Rnds 8–19 Ch 2 (does not count as a st), hdc in each st around; join with sl st in first hdc.

Bobble Band
Note When you turn your work at the beginning of the Set-up Rnd, you will be working on the WS. You'll continue to work only on the WS (NOT turning) until all rnds of the Bobble Band are complete. This becomes the RS when the band is folded up.
Set-up Rnd (WS) Ch 1, *turn*, working in back loops only, sc in each st around; join with sl st in beg ch-1—56 sc.
Rnd 1 Ch 3 (does not count as a st), do *not* turn, *Bobble in next st, dc in next st; rep from * around; join with sl st in top of beg ch-3—28 Bobbles and 28 dc.
Rnd 2 Ch 1, sc in each st around; join with sl st in beg ch-1—56 sc.
Rnd 3 Ch 3 (does not count as a st), *dc in next st, Bobble in next st; rep from * around; join with sl st in top of beg ch-3.
Rnd 4 Rep Rnd 2.
Rnds 5 and 6 Rep Rnds 1 and 2.
Fasten off.

FINISHING
Weave in ends. •

Shell-Stitch Cowl

Easy

MEASUREMENTS
Circumference Approx 48"/122cm
Height Approx 10"/25.5cm

MATERIALS
Yarn
LION BRAND® Scarfie®, 5.3oz/150g balls; each 312yd/285m (acrylic, wool)
• 1 ball in #209 Charcoal/Aqua

Hook
• Size J/10 (6mm) crochet hook, *or size needed to obtain gauge.*

Notions
• Tapestry needle

GAUGE
3 (sc, ch 3, 3 dc) groups = 3¾"/9.5cm using size J/10 (6mm).
TAKE TIME TO CHECK GAUGE.

NOTES
1) Cowl is worked in one piece, then ends are seamed.
2) The stitch pattern is easy to do, but a diagram is provided to clarify the stitches.

COWL
Ch 36.
Row 1 Work 3 dc in 4th ch from hook (3 skipped ch count as beg ch-sp), *sk next 3 ch, (sc, ch 3, 3 dc) in next ch; rep from * to last 4 ch, sk next 3 ch, sc in last ch—you will have 8 (sc, ch 3, 3 dc) groups at the end of this row (counting the beg ch-sp and 3 dc and the last sc as 1 (sc, ch 3, 3 dc) group).
Row 2 Ch 4, turn, 3 dc in 4th ch from hook (3 skipped ch count as beg ch-sp), (sc, ch 3, 3 dc) in each ch-3 sp across to beg ch-sp, sc in beg ch-sp.
Rep Row 2 until piece measures approx 48"/122cm from beg. Fasten off, leaving a long yarn tail for sewing.

FINISHING
Sew short ends of piece together to make Cowl.
Weave in ends. •

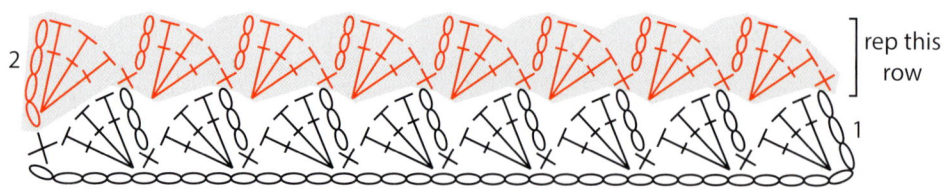